# DISCOVER
# Plants

by Libby Romero

## Table of Contents

# Introduction

**Plants** grow to live. Plants grow in many places.

▲ Plants grow in forests.

▲ Plants grow in gardens.

buds

flowers

leaves

plants

roots

stems

▲ Plants grow at the beach.

See the Glossary on page 22.

3

# What Parts Do Plants Have?

Plants have many parts.

▲ This plant has many parts.

Plants have **leaves**.

▲ This plant has leaves.

Plants have **stems**.

▲ These plants have stems.

leaves

stem

Some plants have **buds**.

▲ This plant has buds.

Some plants have **flowers**.

▲ This plant has flowers.

6

Plants have **roots**.

▲ This plant has roots.

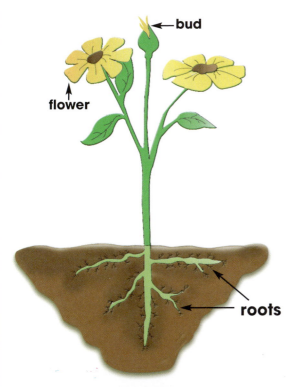

bud

flower

roots

## Try This

1. Look at a plant.
2. Find the parts of the plant.
3. Draw the plant.
4. Label the parts of the plant.

7

# What Do Plants Need to Live?

Plants need water.

▲ These plants need water.

Plants need air.

▲ These plants need air.

Plants need light. Plants need light from the sun.

▲ These plants need light.

Plants need food.

▲ These plants need food.

food

## Did You Know?

Plants make food.
Plants make food
in the leaves.

11

# How Do Plants Grow?

Some plants grow from seeds.

▲ Seeds become plants.

## It's a Fact

People eat seeds. People eat sunflower seeds. People eat pumpkin seeds.

Some plants grow from big seeds.

▲ big seed

▲ Some big seeds become trees.

Some plants grow from little seeds.

▲ little seeds

▲ Little seeds become plants.

Some plants grow from acorns.

▲ acorns

▲ Acorns become trees.

Some plants grow from pinecone seeds.

▲ **pinecones**

▲ **Pinecone seeds become trees.**

Some plants grow from bulbs.

▲ bulbs

▲ Some bulbs become vegetables.

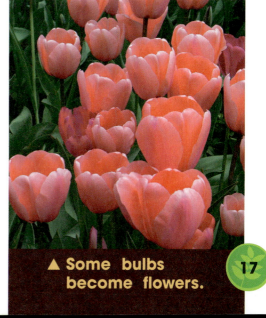

▲ Some bulbs become flowers.

# Conclusion

Plants grow. Plants grow many parts. Many plants grow from seeds.

# Concept Map

## Plants

| What Parts Do Plants Have? | What Do Plants Need to Live? |
| --- | --- |
| leaves | water |
| stems | air |
| buds | light |
| flowers | food |
| roots | |

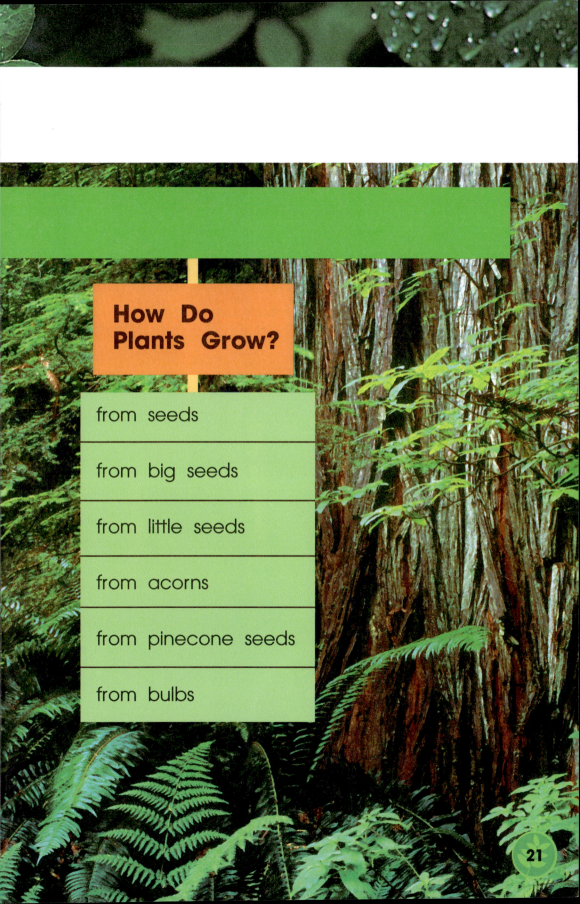

## How Do Plants Grow?

from seeds

from big seeds

from little seeds

from acorns

from pinecone seeds

from bulbs

# Glossary

**buds** the beginning parts of flowers

*Some plants have **buds**.*

**flowers** parts of a plant that make seeds

*Some plants have **flowers**.*

**leaves** flat, green parts of a plant

*Plants have **leaves**.*

**plants** living things that can not move

***Plants** grow in many places.*

**roots** parts of a plant that grow into the ground

*Plants have **roots**.*

**stems** parts of a plant that hold leaves and flowers

*Plants have **stems**.*

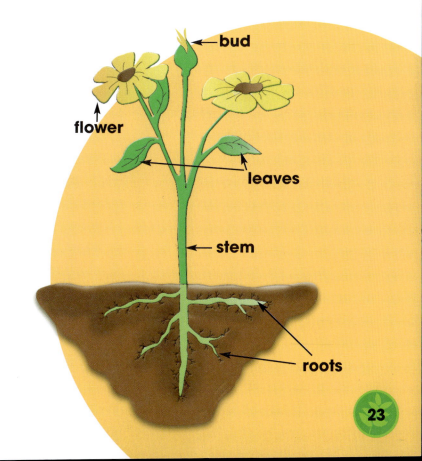

bud

flower

leaves

stem

roots

# Index